Double Bass Solo 1

Fifty melodies selected and adapted by
Keith Hartley

Music Department
OXFORD UNIVERSITY PRESS
Oxford and New York

Contents

DOUBLE BASS SOLO

BOOK 1

Fifty Melodies
selected and adapted by
KEITH HARTLEY

Half Position
or
First Degree

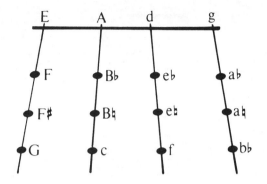

1. THE GREAT GATE OF KIEV

Pictures from an Exhibition

MODEST MUSSORGSKY
(1839 – 81)

2. TORTUES

Le Carnaval des Animaux

CAMILLE SAINT-SAËNS
(1835 – 1921)

3. WALTZ

Roses from the South (Op.388)

JOHANN STRAUSS
(1825 – 99)

The acciaccatura (♪) in bar 13 is played as quickly as possible, eg.

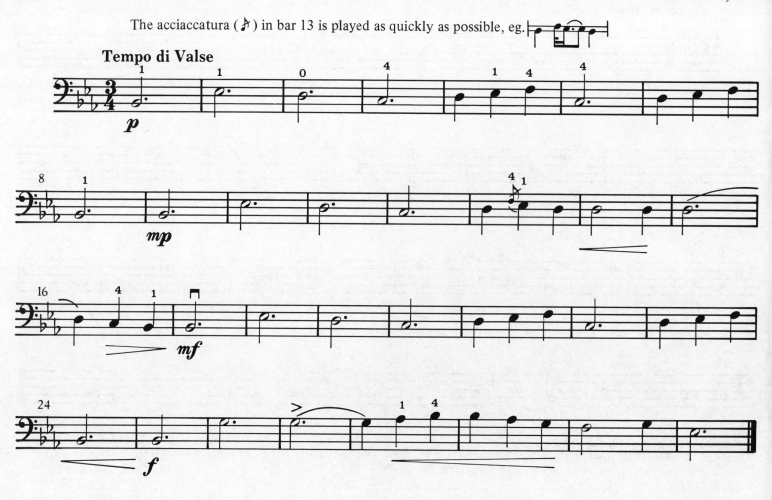

4. CANON ON 'FRÈRE JACQUES'

Symphony 1

GUSTAV MAHLER
(1860 – 1911)

5. THE MERRY PEASANT

Album for the Young (Op.68)

ROBERT SCHUMANN
(1810 – 56)

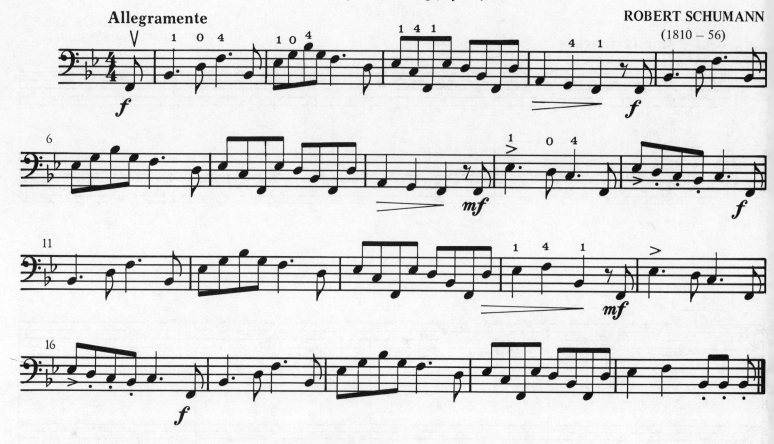

6. ENTR'ACTE

Incidental Music to 'Rosamunde'

FRANZ SCHUBERT
(1797 – 1828)

The g♭ in bar 13 introduces a 'shift' into First Position. Changes of position are easily recognised by the circled fingering. (① indicates the return to Half Position.)

First Position

or

Second Degree

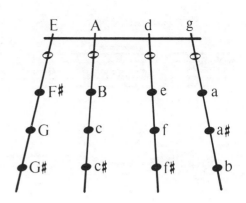

7. ODE TO JOY

Symphony 9 'The Choral'

L.van BEETHOVEN
(1770 – 1827)

8. DRINK TO ME ONLY

ENGLISH AIR
(17th cent.)

9. PILGRIMS' MARCH

Symphony 4 'The Italian'

FELIX MENDELSSOHN
(1809 – 47)

10. MINUET

12 Duets for two Basset Horns (K.487)

W.A. MOZART
(1756 – 91)

11. MINUET
Aires and Dances

JOHN ECCLES
(1660 – 1735)

12. THE TROUT
Variation 3: Piano Quintet (Op.114)

FRANZ SCHUBERT
(1797 – 1828)

Major Scales & Arpeggios

(up to $2\tfrac{1}{2}$ position)

KEY	No. of flats
F	1
B♭	2
E♭	3
A♭	4
D♭	5
G♭	6

C major
has neither
flats nor sharps
in the key signature

KEY	No. of sharps
G	1
D	2
A	3
E	4
B	5
F♯	6

Minor Scales & Arpeggios

(up to 2½ position)

KEY	No. of flats
D	1
G	2
C	3
F	4
B♭	5
E♭	6

A minor
has neither
sharps nor flats
in the key signature

KEY	No. of sharps
E	1
B	2
F♯	3
C♯	4
G♯	5
D♯	6

E harmonic

A harmonic

B harmonic

F♯ harmonic

G melodic

C melodic

C♯ melodic

Second Position
or
Third Degree

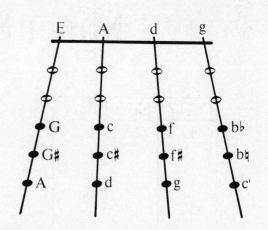

13. ANDANTE CANTABILE
String Quartet 1 (Op.11)
P.I. TCHAIKOVSKY
(1840 – 93)

The notes in Bar 1 should be taken in Second Position and slurred across the string.
To help produce a fine *legato* sound, press the fingers for both notes firmly down together.

14. LULLABY
Op.49 No.4
JOHANNES BRAHMS
(1833 – 97)

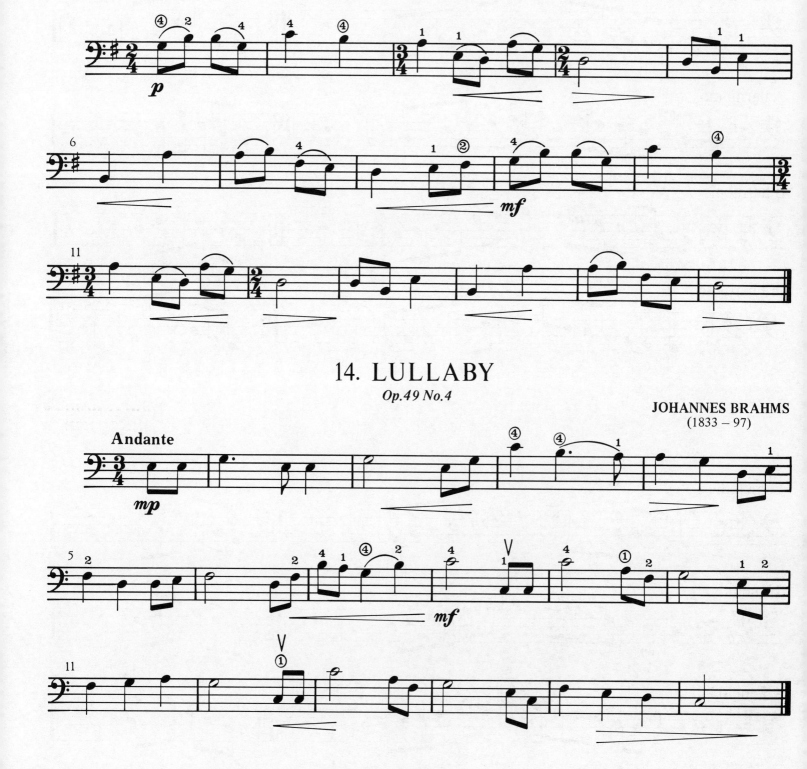

15. MARCH

Judas Maccabaeus

G.F. HANDEL
(1685 – 1759)

16. NOW IS THE MONTH OF MAYING

THOMAS MORLEY
(1557 – 1603)

12

17. OLD FRENCH SONG
Album for the Young

P.I. TCHAIKOVSKY
(1840 – 93)

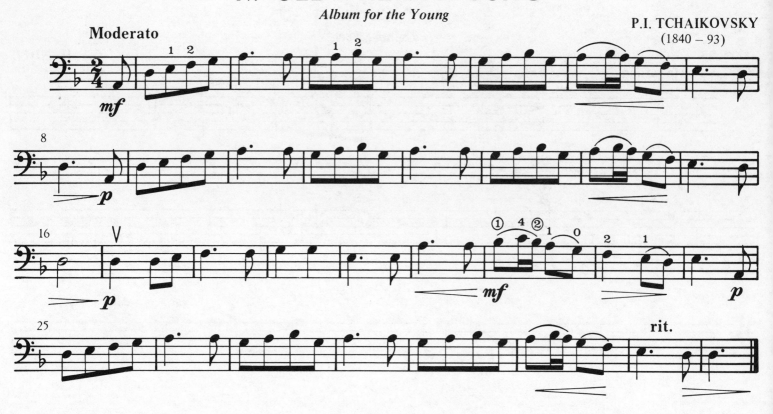

18. BERCEUSE
Dolly Suite (Op.56)

The notes c' and d' in bars 13 and 14 introduce a new 'shift' into Third Position.

GABRIEL FAURÉ
(1845 – 1924)

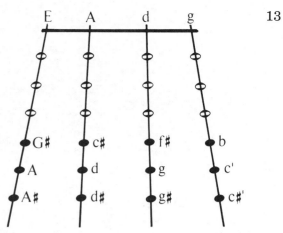

2½ Position

or

Fourth Degree

19. FINLANDIA Op.26 No.7

JEAN SIBELIUS
(1865 – 1957)

A new feature in 2½ Position is the use of a bracket (⌐¬) over a group of notes to indicate that they can now be played, across the string, in one position.

20. THE HARMONIOUS BLACKSMITH

Harpsichord Suite 5 in E

G.F. HANDEL
(1685 – 1759)

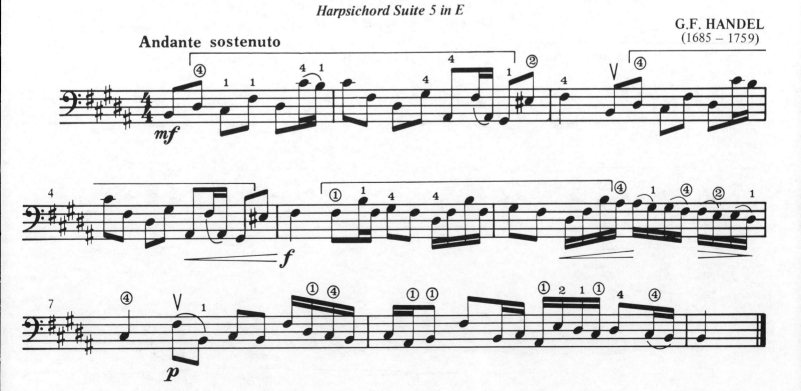

Third Position
or
Fifth Degree
21. MY HEART EVER FAITHFUL
Cantata 68

J.S. BACH
(1685 – 1750)

22. LARGO
Symphony 9 'From the New World'

ANTONIN DVOŘÁK
(1841 – 1904)

In this, originally a solo for Cor Anglais, play the notes ♩♪ as *legato* as possible.

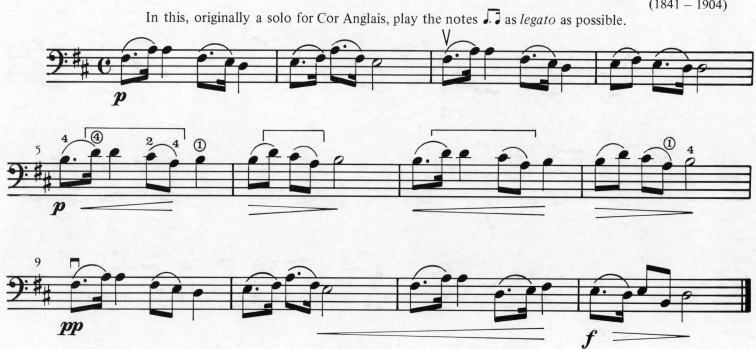

23. MARCH

Scipio

G.F. HANDEL
(1685 – 1759)

Here the same rhythm is played *staccato* , with the notes 'hooked' together in one bow.

24. ANDANTINO

Symphony 4

P.I. TCHAIKOVSKY
(1840 – 93)

16

25. ANDANTE
Variation 6: Rococo Variations (Op.33)

P.I. TCHAIKOVSKY
(1840 – 93)

26. JUPITER
The Planets

GUSTAV HOLST
(1874 – 1934)

27. THE GIFT TO BE SIMPLE

SHAKER SONG
(19th cent.)

28. WHERE'ER YOU WALK

Semele
The notes e' and d' in bars 26-27 introduce a new 'shift' into Fourth Position.

G.F. HANDEL
(1685 – 1759)

29. JESU, JOY OF MAN'S DESIRING

Cantata 147

J.S. BACH
(1685 – 1750)

3½ Position

or

Sixth Degree

30. GREENSLEEVES

Trad. English

31. WHEN I AM LAID IN EARTH

Dido and Aeneas

HENRY PURCELL
(1659 – 95)

This famous example of a 'ground bass' is arranged here as a duet;
the five-bar phrase, first heard alone, is repeated three times under the melody.

32. ANDANTE

Trumpet Concerto

JOSEPH HAYDN
(1732 – 1809)

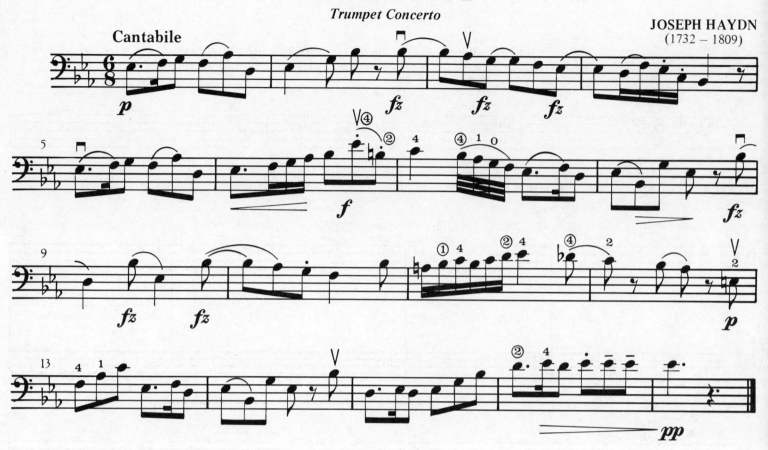

33. MINUET

L'Arlésienne Suite 2

GEORGES BIZET
(1838 – 75)

The g' harmonic in bar 2 can be played by lightly touching
the string with the 3rd finger in Sixth Position.

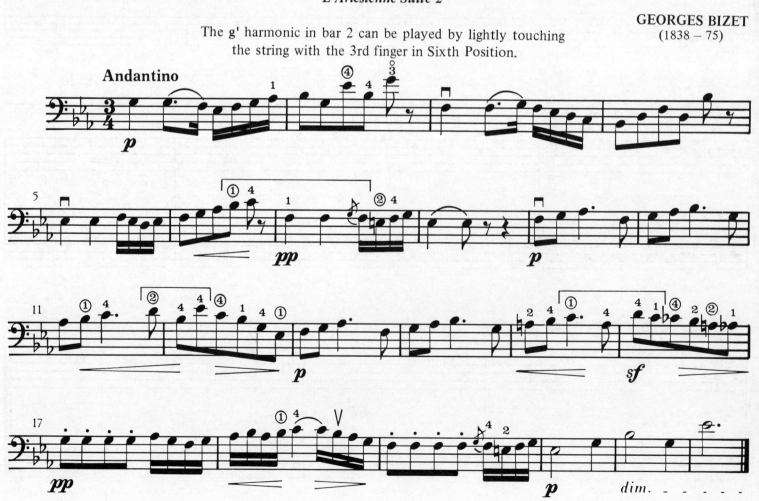

Fourth Position

or

Seventh Degree

34. SHEEP MAY SAFELY GRAZE

Cantata 208

J.S. BACH
(1685 – 1750)

35. POÈME
for Violin and Orchestra (Op.25)

ERNEST CHAUSSON
(1855 – 99)

36. MINUET

L.van BEETHOVEN
(1770 – 1827)

D.C. al Fine

37. RONDO ALL'ONGARESE
Piano Trio in G

JOSEPH HAYDN
(1732 – 1809)

A preparatory exercise: double-stopping in thirds.

The opening bars are fingered in some detail, both to introduce the notes e' and c' in Fifth Position, and to show the value of playing the notes across the string in thirds. *See also No.45, bars 12-16, in Sixth Position.*

Minor Scales & Arpeggios

(up to sixth position)

D melodic

D harmonic

E♭ melodic

E♭ harmonic

E melodic

F harmonic

F# melodic

G harmonic

E arpeggio

F arpeggio

F# arpeggio

G arpeggio

Fifth Position
or
Eighth Degree

38. INTERMEZZO
Cavalleria Rusticana

PIETRO MASCAGNI
(1863 – 1945)

The **a'** harmonic in bar 23 can be played with the 1st Finger in Fourth Position.

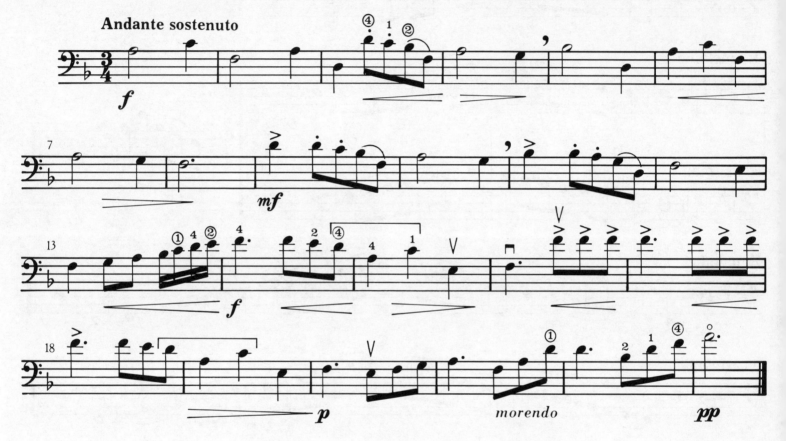

39. TOREADOR'S SONG
Carmen: Act 2 No.14

GEORGES BIZET
(1838 – 75)

40. ST. ANTHONY CHORALE
Haydn Variations

JOHANNES BRAHMS
(1833 – 97)

41. NOCTURNE
A Midsummer Night's Dream

FELIX MENDELSSOHN
(1809 – 47)

42. MINUET
The Anna Magdalena Notebook

J.S. BACH
(1685 – 1750)

5½ Position
or
Ninth Degree

43. PAVANE Op.50

GABRIEL FAURÉ
(1845 – 1924)

Andante molto moderato

44. VALSE

Coppélia: Act 1 No.1

LÉO DELIBES
(1836 – 91)

Sixth Position and Above

or

Tenth Degree

45. ALLEGRO VIVACE

Overture 'Rosamunde'

FRANZ SCHUBERT
(1797 – 1828)

Note the playing of thirds across the string in bars 12-16. *See also No.37.*

46. ENTR'ACTE No.2

Carmen

GEORGES BIZET
(1838 – 75)

The remaining pieces introduce the Thumb Position and Tenor Clef, for which some suggested fingerings are shown below:

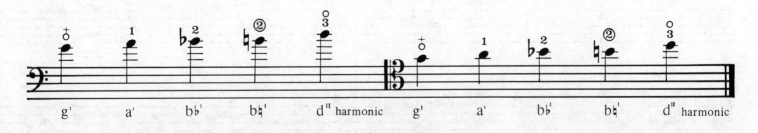

47. AGNUS DEI

Requiem

GIUSEPPE VERDI
(1813 – 1901)

48. PRELUDE

Op.28 No.20

FRÉDÉRIC CHOPIN
(1810 – 49)

Each 4-bar phrase is notated first in the Bass Clef, with the repeat in the Tenor Clef.

49. PRAELUDIUM
after Pugnani

FRITZ KREISLER
(1875 – 1962)

50. SONATINA

L. van BEETHOVEN
(1770 – 1827)

Reproduced and printed by
Halstan & Co. Ltd., Amersham, Bucks., England

Acknowledgements

Acknowledgement is due to the following for permission to include copyright material :

No 2 : Reproduced by permission of
   Editions Durand. S. A.,
   Paris/United Music Publishers Ltd.
Nos 18, 43 : Reproduced by permission of
   Editions Hamelle et Cie.,
   Paris/United Music Publishers Ltd.
No 19 : Breitkopf & Härtel, Wiesbaden
No 38 : Ascherberg, Hopwood & Crew Ltd. (Chappell & Co Ltd.)
No 49 : Schott & Co Ltd.